MW00904251

Godfather, ~ tell me ~ your story

© Copyright - Erika Rossi 2021 - All rights reserved

This publication is protected by copyright. No part of this work may be copied, reproduced or

redistributed in any form without the written consent of the author.

Dear godfather,

✿

I offer you this diary so that you can give me the greatest gift : the gift of your life story and experience.

I know and love the person you are today through your role as a godfather, but I would also like to discover your other facets and the different phases that have marked your life and made you the man you are today.

All you have to do is give me back this diary filled with your most personal thoughts, anecdotes and memories. You can either fill it out with me or do it on your own.

Feel free to skip any question you don't want to answer. They have been thought of to guide your life testimony, and can be completed with your own reflections at the end of the diary and embellished with your most beautiful pictures!

Once you have finished your story, I will keep this memory book carefully and treasure it.

I hope you will take as much pleasure in filling it out as I will in reading it.

Thank you very much

♡

SPECIAL REQUEST

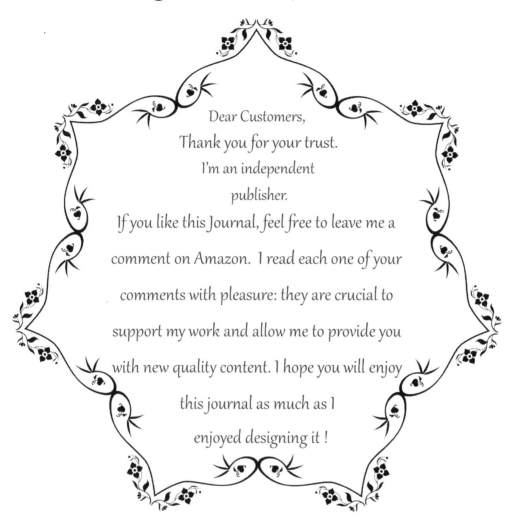

Dear Customers,
Thank you for your trust.
I'm an independent
publisher.
If you like this Journal, feel free to leave me a
comment on Amazon. I read each one of your
comments with pleasure: they are crucial to
support my work and allow me to provide you
with new quality content. I hope you will enjoy
this journal as much as I
enjoyed designing it !

In order not to miss any of my next publications,
I suggest you to scan this QR code and click on
"+ Follow" on my author page :

Thank you very much in advance !

Erika Rossi

SUMMARY

YOU

Your name is

....

How did your parents choose your name ?

....

....

Today; ...., you have .... children, ...
grandchildren and .... great-
grandchildren .

You were born on .... in ....

YOUR ROOTS

(Complete with the names and dates of birth
of your ancestors)

Our best picture

♡

YOUR YOUTH

Did you like going to school ? Did you do well or was it hard for you ?

_____
_____
_____
_____
_____
_____
_____
_____

What were your favorite and least favorite subjects ? Are there any subjects that don't exist anymore ?

_____
_____
_____
_____
_____
_____
_____
_____
_____

Who were your favorite teachers and why ?

Who were your best friends ? What are your best memories with them ?

What did you play in the playground ?

When you misbehaved, how were you punished ? How often were you punished ?

As a child, what was the job you wanted to do when you grew up ?

_____

_____

_____

_____

What were your favorite games/toys ?
How did you spend your free time ?

_____

_____

_____

_____

_____

How did your parents describe you ?

_____

_____

_____

_____

_____

_____

Did you have pets ? If not, do you wish you had ?

What was your nickname ? Why did they call you that ?

What did you do during school vacation ?
If you went away, who did you go with and where ?

What was the biggest mistake you made as a child ?

....
....
....
....
....
....
....
....

What was your favorite book ?

....
....

What was your favorite food ? What was your least favorite food ?

....
....

Tell me the funniest memory of your childhood.

....
....
....
....
....
....
....
....
....

Did you help a lot at home ? What did you do ?

Which birthday is your most special memory ?

Did you have any special family traditions ? What were the family celebrations like and which ones did you prefer ?

What are the happiest memories of your childhood ?

A picture of you as a child ♡

A picture of you as a child ♡

As a teenager, what did you do with your friends ? Did you go out a lot? Did you keep your childhood friends ?

Overall, did you enjoy your adolescence ? What are your best memories ?

Have you pursued your studies ? If so, what did you study ?

Une photo de toi adolescent ♡

YOUR FAMILY

Tell me about your parents : what were their jobs ? Describe their habits and their respective characters. What memories do you have with them ?

Your mom :

_____
_____
_____
_____
_____
_____
_____
_____
_____
_____
_____
_____
_____
_____
_____
_____

Your dad :

A picture of your parents ♡

What did your grandparents do and what were they like ?
How often did you see them ? What did you like to do with
them or at their house ? Did they teach you anything ?

A picture of your maternal grandparents ♡

A picture of your paternal grandparents ♡

What do you know about your great-grandparents and more distant ancestors ?
Does your family have a particular ethnic background ? Are there any stories/legends about your ancestors' bloodline ?

If you have brothers and sisters, what are their names ?
What is your relationship with them like ? Are there any
memorable stories about them ?

Where did you live with your family and what was your home like ?

A picture of your whole family ♡

YOUR ADULTHOOD

As a young adult, what were your best skills ? Which were you best at ?

_____

_____

_____

_____

_____

_____

_____

What principles passed on by your parents have guided your adult life ?

_____

_____

_____

_____

_____

_____

What jobs did you have ? Did you enjoy them ? If you could have started over, would you have chosen the same work ?

_____

_____

_____

Have you ever been on a long journey ? Where did you travel
? What are your favorite travel memories ?

Have you gone through particularly difficult times in your life ?
How did you cope with them ? Did you experience historical
moments when you were younger (war, crisis...) ?

Tell me : when and how did you meet your current partner ?

Tell me more about her (/him).

How many serious relationships have you had in your life ?
What can you tell me about them ?

How did you know that your current relationship was
special ?

If you are married : how did the proposal go ?

_____
_____
_____
_____
_____
_____

What was your wedding like ?
Did you go on honeymoon afterwards ?

_____
_____
_____
_____
_____
_____
_____
_____
_____
_____
_____

If you are a dad : how did you decide to have a child ?

_____
_____
_____
_____
_____

What is your best memory with your partner ?

A picture of both of you ♡

3

At what age did you get your driver's licence ? And your first car? Do you have a funny story about it ?

What is the best gift you have ever received ?

Have you participated in any contests or competitions in your life ?

_____
_____
_____
_____
_____
_____
_____
_____
_____

How has your perception and experience of masculinity evolved over the years ? What makes you feel like a "man" today ?

_____
_____
_____
_____
_____
_____
_____
_____
_____
_____
_____

YOUR LIFE AS A DAD

How did you react when you found out your partner was pregnant ? What about her ?

What was her first pregnancy like ? What about childbirth ? How did you live them ?

How was your first year of fatherhood ?

How did you balance your family life and work obligations ? If you could have started over, would you have done it the same way ?

What did (/do) you enjoy doing most with your children ?

How did you choose your children's names ? Do they have a particular meaning? What were your other favorite names ?

What was the biggest mistake your children made ?

Is there anything you experienced when you were younger that you promised yourself you wouldn't put your own children through ?

What do you like the most about being a dad ?

4

What is the most tiring / difficult thing about being a dad ?

What are you most beautiful memories with your kids ?

Pictures of you ♡

YOUR LIFE AS A GODFATHER

How did you meet your mom and dad ? What is your relationship
with them like ? Why did they choose you as godmother ?

What do you remember about my baptism ?

What is your favorite part of being a godfather ?

What are your favorite activities to do with me ?

Are there things about me that remind you of yourself? Do we have anything in common?

Is there anything you've always wanted to tell me?

What are you most beautiful memories with me ?

Pictures of us ♡

5

YOUR CURRENT LIFE

What are your current favorite activities ?

_____
_____
_____
_____
_____
_____
_____
_____
_____
_____

What are your daily rituals ?

_____
_____
_____
_____
_____
_____
_____
_____

Who are the people you feel closest to today ?

Is there anything I don't know about you that would surprise me ?

What are your favorite books and writers ?

What are your favorite movies and actors ?

What are your favorite music styles and singers ?

If you won the lottery tomorrow, what would you do ?
(You can let your imagination run wild !)

What would you do if you only had one day left to live ?

Are there any skills / knowledge you would like to learn ?

According to you, what are the inventions that have most revolutionized the course of humankind ?

You and your relatives now ♡

RETROSPECTIVE OF YOUR LIFE

Where did you like living the most and why ? Would you have liked to live somewhere else ?

Do you think the world has changed a lot since you were born ? What has surprised you the most ?

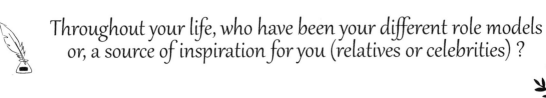

Throughout your life, who have been your different role models or, a source of inspiration for you (relatives or celebrities) ?

What are you most proud of? What experiences have been the most important in your life and have made you the person you are today?

Do you have any regrets ? Do you wish you had done things differently ? What do you wish you had spent less time on ? What about more time on ?

What dreams have you achieved ? Are there any particular things you would like to accomplish ?

How do you imagine your retirement ? If you are already retired, what do you prefer in this phase of your life ?

What are the happiest events and memories in your life ?

What would you like to be remembered for ? What values are most important to you ? What legacy would you like to leave ?

What advice would you give me regarding my personal and professional life ?

I'D ALSO LIKE TO KNOW...

Your favorites tips & recipes

Your favorites tips & recipes

Your favorites tips & recipes

Your favorites tips & recipes

Your favorites tips & recipes

Your favorites tips & recipes

Your favorites tips & recipes

A little love note ...

From me to you :

From you to me :

Your life in pictures ♡

Your life in pictures ♡

Your life in pictures ♡

Your life in pictures ♡

Your life in pictures ♡

Your life in pictures ♡

Your life in pictures ♡

Your life in pictures ♡

Your life in pictures ♡

Your life in pictures ♡

Your life in pictures ♡

Your life in pictures ♡

Your life in pictures ♡

Your life in pictures ♡

Your life in pictures ♡

Your life in pictures ♡

EXTRA NOTES

ALSO AVAILABLE ON AMAZON.COM
-ERIKA ROSSI-

« TELL ME YOUR STORY » COLLECTION

Grandma tell me your story : Keepsake memory journal to be filled by your grandmother with the story of her life

Grandpa tell me your story : Keepsake memory journal to be filled by your grandfather with the story of his life

Dad tell me your story : Keepsake memory journal to be filled by your father with the story of his life

Mom tell me your story : Keepsake memory journal to be filled by your mother with the story of her life

Godmother tell me your story : Keepsake memory journal to be filled by your godmother with the story of her life

Uncle tell me your story : Keepsake memory journal to be filled by your uncle with the story of his life

Aunt tell me your story : Keepsake memory journal to be filled by your auntie with the story of her life

« GRATITUDE JOURNALS » COLLECTION

Lamaste - Gratitude journal for Kids : 3 minute Daily Journal Writing Prompts for Children to practice Gratitude & Mindfulness with Positive Affirmations, Quotes & Challenges

Made in the USA
Monee, IL
08 December 2024

50e7f953-2fa5-4dd6-91e3-648f1211ca35R01